Where Does the Recycling Go?

By Jerry Shea

Gareth Stevens
Publishing

Please visit our website, www.garethstevens.com. For a free color catalog of all our high-quality books, call toll free 1-800-542-2595 or fax 1-877-542-2596.

Library of Congress Cataloging-in-Publication Data

Shea, Jerry, 1954-
Where does the recycling go? / Jerry Shea.
  p. cm. — (Everyday mysteries)
Includes index.
ISBN 978-1-4339-6335-3 (pbk.)
ISBN 978-1-4339-6336-0 (6-pack)
ISBN 978-1-4339-6333-9 (library binding)
1. Recycling (Waste, etc.)—Juvenile literature. 2. Waste products—Juvenile literature. I. Title.
TD794.5.S479 2012
628.4'458—dc23
                              2011036596

First Edition

Published in 2012 by
Gareth Stevens Publishing
111 East 14th Street, Suite 349
New York, NY 10003

Designer: Katelyn E. Reynolds
Editor: Greg Roza

Photo credits: Cover, pp. 1, 7, 11, 13, 19, 21, (pp. 3–24 background and graphics) Shutterstock.com; p. 5 iStockphoto/Thinkstock; p. 9 Chip Chipman/Bloomberg via Getty Images; p. 15 S. Meltzer/PhotoLink/Getty Images; p. 17 CP Cheah/Flickr/Getty Images.

Printed in the United States of America

CPSIA compliance information: Batch #CW12GS: For further information contact Gareth Stevens, New York, New York at 1-800-542-2595.

Contents

Boldface words appear in the glossary.

What Is Recycling?

More than half the garbage gathered in the United States ends up in **landfills**. We can cut the garbage in landfills by recycling. Recycling means sending some kinds of garbage to places where they can be prepared to be used again.

landfill

5

What Can We Recycle?

Recyclable garbage includes paper, metal, glass, and plastic. These things must be sorted before they can be **processed**. Sometimes people sort their recyclable garbage before putting it out. Sometimes it's sorted after it's taken away.

WE
RECYCLE

7

To the Recycling Center!

Garbage workers pick up recyclable garbage and put it on a truck. The truck takes it to a recycling center. At the center, workers sort the garbage into the different groups. What happens next depends on the kind of garbage.

Paper

Paper is **shredded** and mixed with water. The mix is cleaned to remove things like plastic and glue. Then it's sprayed onto a flat surface and heated. As it dries, it forms new paper. The new paper is rolled up.

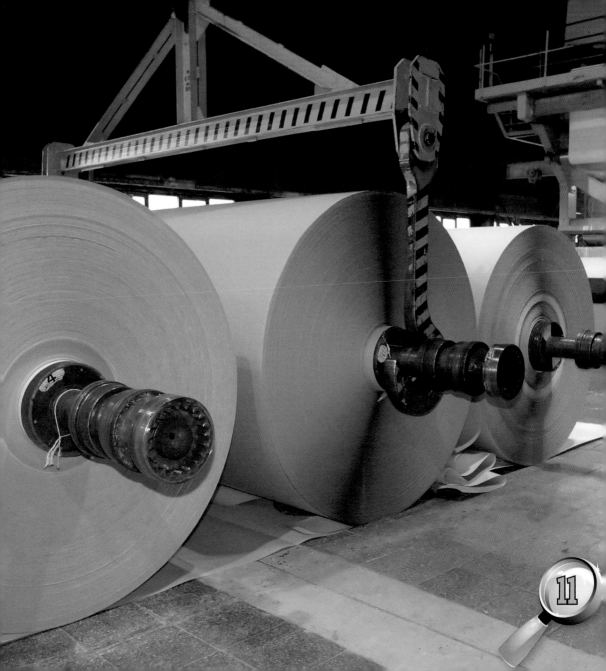

Metal

Most metals are recycled the same way. Aluminum cans are crushed and shredded. Then they're melted in a **furnace**. The liquid is poured into molds. After it hardens, it's rolled flat. New cans are made from the recycled aluminum.

Glass

At a glass recycling center, glass is sorted into clear, green, and brown groups. The glass is cleaned and crushed. It's melted in a furnace and shaped into new bottles and jars. Sometimes bottles are cleaned and reused without melting them.

Glass

Brown Glass
↓

Green Glass
↓

Clear Glass
↓

Plastic

Plastics are sorted by type and shredded. The plastic is cleaned to remove things like paper and glue, and then dried. Next, it's melted and shaped into tiny balls called nurdles. Nurdles are melted and formed into new plastic goods.

16

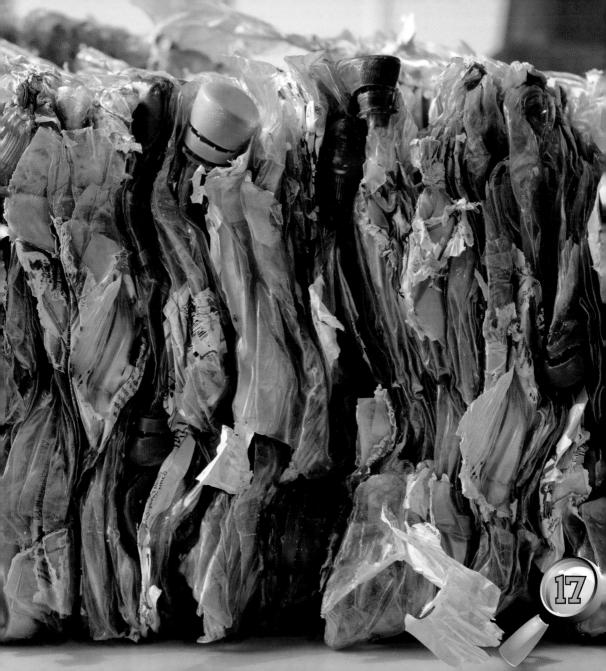

Special Garbage

Some things can't be taken to a regular recycling center. Old tires and batteries are very bad for the **environment**. They need to go to special recycling centers. TVs and computers must go to special recycling centers, too.

18

Why Should We Recycle?

Recycling helps the environment. Plastic and glass don't break down like food does. They stay in landfills for thousands of years. Recycling also saves **resources** and keeps the environment cleaner by using less **energy**.

Facts About Recycling

RECYCLING CENTER

Metal

A used aluminum can is recycled into a new can and is in a store in just 60 days.

Paper

Recycling 1 ton (0.9 mt) of paper saves 17 trees.

Glass

Glass takes up to 4,000 years to break down in a landfill, but it can be recycled over and over.

Plastic

In 2009, 2,456,000 pounds (1,115,000 kg) of plastic bottles were recycled in the United States.

Glossary

energy: power used to do work

environment: the natural world

furnace: a closed place where heat is produced

landfill: a place where garbage is buried

process: to move something forward in a set of steps. Also, the set of steps itself.

resource: a usable supply of something

shred: to tear into small pieces

For More Information

Books

Goldsmith, Mike. *Recycling*. New York, NY: Crabtree Publishing, 2010.

Inches, Alison. *The Adventures of a Plastic Bottle: A Story About Recycling*. New York, NY: Little Simon, 2009.

Nelson, Sara E. *Let's Reduce Garbage!* Mankato, MN: Capstone Press, 2007.

Websites

Earth911
earth911.com
Learn more about recycling and find recycling centers near you.

Reduce, Reuse, and Recycle
kids.niehs.nih.gov/recycle.htm
Learn more about recycling and how to reduce the amount of garbage you make.

Index